TO QUIERRA, ON LIFE

Glenora Wells-Sanders (Afi)

Bloomington, IN  Milton Keynes, UK

authorHOUSE®

AuthorHouse™
1663 Liberty Drive, Suite 200
Bloomington, IN 47403
www.authorhouse.com
Phone: 1-800-839-8640

AuthorHouse™ UK Ltd.
500 Avebury Boulevard
Central Milton Keynes, MK9 2BE
www.authorhouse.co.uk
Phone: 08001974150

First published by AuthorHouse 4/23/2007

ISBN: 978-1-4259-9064-0 (sc)

*Printed in the United States of America
Bloomington, Indiana*

This book is printed on acid-free paper.

Dedication Page

I first dedicate this book to my mom, Catherine Chandler, whose spirit of love, strength, compassion, and perseverance lives on in me.

I secondly dedicate this book to my sister Doris, who was always my number-one fan. I know she still smiles on me in heaven.

I thirdly dedicate this book to my son Tony, whom I love and adore so very much. You have made me so very proud of you.

And lastly I dedicate this book to all of the grandmothers and granddaughters who appreciate my time and effort in this endeavor.

Introduction Page:

Dear Quierra,

I often wished when growing up that my mother, sister, or aunts would have told me in certain detail some of the lessons in life I had to painfully learn on my own. So I made a solemn vow that if my son ever had a daughter, I would not only share those things that bring hurts and disappointments, but I would also share those things that would make life much fuller and richer. I have been in great contemplation since the blessing of your birth on May 18, 1988 of what I would actually say to you about life. So, on this twenty-first day of October 1997, I begin the task.

Each time I looked into your beautiful and innocent eyes, I felt a sense of sadness because of what I know I cannot save you from as you embark upon your own personal journey of life. You may ask, Why write this book then? What is the urgency of the matter?

There is no urgency. I write to you solely out of love and in the hopes that you will gain some values and insights I so often wished were shared by the great matriarchs in my life. I now understand their silence. I have done all right in spite of it. I still hold my matriarchs in the highest regard. But I cannot and will not be silent with you. Please take what you need from these words. Do with them what you please. Hopefully your life will somehow be better and richer from the knowledge that is imparted.

Love,
Cookie, your grandmother

Table of Contents

CHAPTER I
The Source Within

Yes, my darling, right now, wherever you are or whatever you endeavor to do in life, take comfort in knowing that you are not alone. You see, your total being is not only physical, which means what you know of yourself from the outside. You are also a spiritual being. You have an inner being that has been a part of you from the time you were born to this present day.

Oftentimes we as human beings don't have this awareness until later in life. And that's because we too often live from the outside-in instead of from the inside-out. We too often get caught up in so many aspects of our physical selves, making it difficult for our inner beings (that source within) to be awakened, to connect. We get too consumed with being too tall or too short, too dark or too light. We worry about our hair being too thin or too thick, or if we have big breasts or no breasts, big hips or no hips, big legs or skinny legs, crooked teeth or gapped teeth. And we go on and on and on.

I can remember times in my life when I felt most inadequate because I was too skinny, too light, too cute, or not cute enough. There were times when I hated to show my face in public because my acne had more eruptions than any volcanic eruptions I learned about in geography class. There were a lot of things about myself that I did not like. Don't get me wrong now, the outer being—our physical attributes—do play a large part in how we feel about ourselves. For when we look good we very often feel good. What is important to remember is that your physical attributes (the way you see yourself) are meaningless if you are not in touch with your inner being, that source within, the true essence of your being.

You see, that source within is your God-self. It is your Divine Nature. That source within builds your character in a way that your outer, physical self could never do. That source within does not feel compelled to measure up to the superficial standards of our Western culture. That source gives you a sense of peace. It tells you that "Lo, I am with you always, even until the end of time" (Mat. 4-28).

That source within allows you to forgive yourself for whatever mistakes in life you have made and will continue to make. That source within tells you that you can be an astronaut, doctor, nurse, teacher, or president if you dare to try. Your source helps you to give comfort, love, and understanding to those who feel loss and despair. Your source within allows you to ask for forgiveness from those you have wronged. And it allows you to forgive those who have wronged, offended, or hurt you until your heart seemed broken into a thousand pieces.

The source within helps you to accept your failures and the failures of others. It also keeps you glued together when you don't get that man you want, that promotion you were entitled to, that house, car, or some other material possession you desired so. The source tells you that when one door closes, a new one always opens. And guess what? Behind that new door is the better man, the better promotion or job, the better house or car. That's because the source within teaches you to be still and wait—wait patiently. It teaches you that being consumed by jealousy, anger, or bitterness blocks the good that is awaiting you. The source within helps you to know that you are a child of the universe, an heir to a great kingdom. You deserve to have the best life offers.

The source within helps you to make it through the saddest and most difficult times in your life, for there will be times when the people who have been most special to you move on to another life. And when this happens, you will be faced with the realization that these special ones will no longer be around to laugh with you, cry with you, nurture, and comfort you. You will no longer see their smiles, be held by them, be encouraged, and more importantly, be understood. It is then when your inner source becomes your anchor, your alpha and your omega. It teaches you that one day in spirit we will all be reunited. So we learn to move forward, carrying in our hearts the many wonderful things we learned from these special ones. And more importantly, we share those important lessons with those we meet in our journeys. The source teaches us that.

By now, you may be asking, how do I awaken the source within? How do I get in touch with my inner nature? How long do I wait to hear the voice that guides me, comforts me, and encourages me? You see, my darling, that is your own personal challenge.

I cannot give you the answer. What I will do is give you some suggestions that will help activate your inner source, the reservoir of help available to you.

1. Give thanks

    Take time out every day to give thanks, for the source within appreciates your humility and blesses you abundantly when it is acknowledged.

2. Service

    Do something positive for someone each and every day of your life. Something positive could be simple acts of kindness, such as a smile to a stranger, a word of comfort and encouragement, or perhaps a monetary gift to a charitable cause. Or it could be something of a greater magnitude: volunteering in a nursing home, hospice, prison, community center, or an outreach program in your church. Just remember that service activates your source within and provides you with a sense of well-being that cannot be compared to anything external.

3. Seek

    Seek to know your inner truths, your higher power. Read, write down your inner-most thoughts, and get in touch with the magnificent being that you are. Your source within is often the only true friend around. The sooner you connect with it, the easier life challenges will be.

4. Come ye apart a while

    Take time out to get away with yourself each day. Those times will serve to be most valuable, for you will be renewed, rejuvenated, and revived. You may quietly get away early in the morning, sometime during the midday, or perhaps at the end of your day. You will also need a special place to get away to, your own personal sanctuary. Just remember that you first have to be comfortable in spending time with yourself before you can ever spend effective time with others.

5. Be orderly

    Order transcends in your life. Start by tidying your surroundings. Get rid of those *things* that block your flow. In order to activate that source within, you have to clean up the mess around you. Get organization in your affairs. If you fail to plan, you plan to fail. Structure is a part of the organizing process. Write down your long-term and short-term goals and do everything in your power to achieve them. Then call on your higher source to work in all of your endeavors. It always knows what's best.

I was around twenty-two when I began to really understand my reservoir of strength, the source within. I had recently walked away from a marriage that was doomed from the start. I knew that life was not going to be easy as a single mom. Still, it was the only choice I had at the time. Your father - my son, and I moved into a large boarding house in Baltimore City. Although I had the love and support of some family members and friends, I felt so frightened and extremely alone.

Not long after my move into the boarding house, another male boarder took residence as a tenant. I learned later that this individual had severe mental problems and should not have taken residence in this type of setting, particularly one that was occupied by a single woman like me. One night in December he broke down the door to my bedroom with the mindset to rape me. Your father at that time was around two years old. I can still hear his piercing cries as he watched this deranged person attempting to strangle and beat the life out of me. Each time I attempted to run out of the house with my son, he would grab me from the back and continue his attack.

My final attempt to free myself was to break the glass window of the home we resided in to get the attention of anyone passing by. And I did. I broke the window with my bare hands and screamed for attention. It was a cold, rainy night. A couple turned around when they heard the glass break and my screams. I was then knocked to the floor.

The room began to darken around me. I remember not being able to breathe. And then I once again heard the piercing cries of my son. I believe that had it not been for those cries of distress, I would not have had the strength to fight my attacker. I also believe that at that time an inner strength, my source within, was crying out. I believe it told me to "fight for your life, fight for your place on the planet, for there is so much here for you to do." The police came and arrested this deranged man.

The trip to the hospital felt like an out-of-body experience. I vaguely recall the ER physician discussing the lacerations on my neck. My head began to spin from all of the questions, both from the ER and the police officers taking down the report. When my sister

Doris showed, I sobbed uncontrollably. She assured me that my son Tony was safe, and she promised she would be with me to see this tragedy to the end.

Yes, I miraculously survived this ordeal. My attacker did not succeed in his attempt to both rape and kill me. I was not seriously injured on the outside. I was, however, emotionally and mentally wrecked. I was tired of the hard blows life had set before me. The day I chose to move from the boarding house where the incident had occurred was a turning point for me. I casually picked up a magazine as I awaited the movers. I don't quite remember why or how I took notice of an article written by Marilyn McCoo of the group known as the Fifth Dimension. I just remember becoming very interested in the words she had written.

She spoke candidly about her life and some of the sad and difficult situations that she had experienced. But more importantly, she encouraged her readers to think positively about life. She urged us not to feel sorry for ourselves, not to wallow in self-pity. She discovered that when she changed her mind about how she viewed life, so many things about life began to change for her. She was a survivor, and she helped me and I'm sure so many others become survivors also. She will never know how she impacted my life.

But that's what your inner strength will do for you. It will help you through others. Your revelation may come from a religious person or it may not. It does not have to be from a parent or teacher, but it could be. But rest assured, something or someone is out there, ready and willing to help you see the light, to make that connection.

I have had many more challenges and roadblocks since that time in my life. And I have not always been right in the decisions regarding my life. But what I do know is that I am much stronger and more powerful than I've ever imagined myself to be. I now know that I am loved by the universe and that I am unique in what have to give to it. The source within has told me so, and I believe it to be true.

God speed.

CHAPTER II
Parents

It was my first real part in a school play. I had to leave for school earlier than usual that morning because we were to meet in the auditorium and be assembled before the start of the performance. I was in the third grade and was the second youngest child in our family of six. I had a very insignificant role in that play as I think back. I was just an ice skater. Yet for days I practiced the moves we were instructed to do on stage in my stocking feet.

On the morning of the play my mom had my long socks waiting for me. She seemed to know just how important it was to have them ready and on time. She must have also sensed how nervous I was about my debut performance because she made arrangements with my father to watch my younger sister so she could attend the play. The time arrived. All of us skaters were given the cue to slide around on stage. I took one nervous look out into the audience and saw my mother coming in. Such a wave of relief came over me. I no longer felt frightened, and I skated to the music as if I were the only one on stage.

As I think back on that memory I am reminded of what vital roles parents play in our lives. I don't think we really realize the extent we shape, mold, and sculpt the beings you become. That is because parenting, my darling, is one of the most difficult of all responsibilities one could ever have in his or her life. The magnitude of all that is required is far beyond anything that I have ever imagined. Just remember that we as parents stumble through this job. Sometimes it seems as though we have all the answers to your whys and our why not. Then some unexpected circumstance arrives (by you, the son or daughter, no doubt) and we have little or no clue to resolving it. Even the best parenting or psychology books are useless. I cannot even be so bold as to express to you what impact your parents will have on your life. I just pray that they will give you the right stuff to help you grow into a well-balanced and productive member of society. I hope that somehow you will want to make a difference in the world.

I don't attempt to kid you about the fact that all parents are good parents. They are not. You will encounter friends who have parents that seem to take no interest in their well-being. Some will be fathers; some will be mothers. And in some cases both parents will lack the necessary skills of parenting. I think mothers, more often than fathers, however, really get lost in the whole process of parenting. And if I had to sum up the whole process into just two words, I would say parenting means love and sacrifice.

I don't believe a day went by in those two years I was hospitalized without a visit from my father or mother. The two facilities I stayed in were very far away because of the nature of my illness. The only means of transportation my parents had at that time was the bus, which only went part of the way. The other mile or two was walked by my mother or father. Still, their desire to visit their child was not deterred.

It was so hard for me and the other children to see our parents leave after a visit. A visit never went by without one of us crying to go home with our parents. Sometimes we would cry all night. I never knew until later on in life how difficult it was for my parents to leave after a visit. I also learned why my parents never visited without a Hershey Bar. They knew this distraction could stop my tears. As they expressed to me later, the sight of my tears tore deeply into their hearts and left them with such a sense of sorrow and despair. "Poor Cookie," my father would say as he made his long way back home. "Poor little Cookie."

The depth of love we have and the sacrifices we make as parents cannot be matched. And when you hurt, we hurt. How we choose to express our love is what I believe gets us into situations that oftentimes do more damage than good. As parents we very often let our love get in the way of sound judgment, and this often impedes your growth. As children and young adults, you take our love and sacrifices for granted. The end result of these actions very often leads to conflict, and you will have some conflict at one time or another with your parents, Quierra.

Your conflict may be the friends you choose, your style of dressing, your grades in school, or some behavior of your parents. Just remember that underneath all of the conflict, your parents do love you. What most parents want is to be loved back. And we do more and give more so that you will show us that you do care about all of the sacrifices we make on your behalf. So strive to be the best you can be for your parents.

I cried all day when I received confirmation of my pregnancy. I could not at that time understand why my mom was so elated. We kept the news from my father for seven months. My dad reacted as we expected, so to keep from bringing shame on my family, I was forced into a shotgun wedding. So there I was: pregnant, married, and a college dropout at the age of nineteen.

I have learned a lot since that time in my life. The task of parenting is time-consuming. That is why I chose to only have one child. And I want you to keep this in mind as well. When we decide to have children and we are young in our patterns of behaviors, our children suffer in some way. They may not be deprived of the material things, but they are deprived during their developmental stages. This is because as young parents we still want to have some fun in life. And whether we want to admit it or not, our kids tend to get in the way of our fun.

When I say *fun*, I don't necessarily mean partying from dusk to dawn. I mean coming and going with little accountability to anyone. I mean being able to take a trip without having to worry about who would be willing to watch your child while you are away. I mean spending the remainder of your paycheck on your own necessities. And if by some unfortunate plight the task of parenting is incumbent upon you alone, when you do meet someone, the hope is that he or she will want your child to be a part of his or her life. Our children feel our sense of frustration. They know inwardly that they have become a burden, and they act out on those feelings.

You have experienced a major crisis with the breakup of your mom and dad. I could see it in your persona. I was very saddened when you made your statement in West Virginia that your mother and father's breakup was one of the saddest times in your life. I wish I could have touched that part in your heart and filled it with love. But I knew I could not. Time has a way of healing all of our hurts. Just understand that you were not to blame. It was never an easy subject to talk about, especially since my son, your dad, stood out as the main culprit in the demise of the marriage.

I pray that a healing will come between them. It is necessary for a healthy existence. Just keep in mind that when you make a decision to take someone as a partner for life, you may never be prepared for the actions and behaviors of that person.

I try not to have many regrets about the course of my life. But I can speak to the fact of how a young man feels without his father's love and guidance. This is so pervasive in our African American community. I thought I could be enough for my son. Yet I wanted to enjoy life, and in my pursuit of career endeavors he did suffer. I now know that. His father passed away a few years ago. He will never be able to make up the time absent from his son. I am grateful that God has allowed me to be there for my son, your dad, at one of his lowest and darkest times in his adult life. You see, parenting never ends.

So, my darling, the lesson here is to wait. Your children deserve to have two loving parents who are mature in their thinking, grounded in their own beings, and willing to place you before anything and everything else in life. These prerequisites may not guarantee the kind of son or daughter you hope to have, but they will give your child the kind of start in life so many of our children never have. I am thankful for the kind of upbringing I received from my parents, in spite of some of the conflicts.

I now know why my mother was happy about the birth of my son, your father. I believe that she felt as I did about this new role. As a grandparent, you have the gift of wisdom. You know what you need to do to get where you need to go. And you do it with such panache! I am a young grandparent, as many of us are today. I have to admit, the initial phone call made to me by your grandma that my son was going to be a father was not met with a lot of enthusiasm. However, I accepted this new role and decided that I would be there for you in whatever way I could. I miss my mom and dad. Each day I encounter something that brings to my mind some memory of them. So I say to you, my darling, love, respect, and cherish your parents while you have them. And endeavor to be the best you can for them, for me, and more importantly, for yourself.

Grandma Love

CHAPTER III

Self-Love

To know thy-self is to love thy-self. If you don't love yourself, no one will. You have to be comfortable with who you are before you can be comfortable with anyone. These are such great words of wisdom from great minds about self-love, loving your-self. This is a difficult chapter for me, as is the chapter on love, sex, and relationships. I too am still discovering and rediscovering myself. I like to think that I am still a work in progress. And because I am still a work in progress, I am still trying to determine what it means to love oneself, to have self-love.

You live in a time when your male counterparts, through their rap lyrics for instance, devalue your worth as women. They speak and sing of their experiences of women in such a negative manner. You are referred to as "bitches", "hos," and "lesbos." The general consensus of the adults who interact with you is that you are a lost generation. They feel that you have few values and you have little thought about future consequences. With so much negativity, how in the world can you know the true worth of yourself? How can you have self-love?

I like to believe that when I look into my mirror each day, I see past what everyone else sees. I see the reflection of some wrong choices, wrong thoughts, and wrong behaviors. Yet I can still love me and embrace me in the time I am presently in.

I feel that in loving yourself, you have to be able to understand yourself and why you act, think, and behave in the way you do. You have to be truly honest with yourself. And this is so difficult because so much of how we act, think, and believe is influenced by so many of the people who are responsible for raising us. These are people like our parents, grandparents, aunts, uncles, teachers, and people who enculturate us. More often than not, these people have not always done a great job in teaching us about self-love.

We are also influenced by our peers, the people we see each day at school or the people we just hang out with. And I cannot leave out those special people, like our significant others. They are the ones we share our most intimate times with, disclosing our most intimate thoughts.

So as you can see, there are many, many voices. With so many voices describing who we are, it is no wonder we have so many uncertainties about ourselves. We hear their voices. We hear them in the still of the night. We hear them when we look in the mirror. We hear them when we are walking alone. Some of these voices have helped us feel good about ourselves—about whom we are and what we have accomplished.

Other voices and conversations have hurt us to the core. They are the ones that make us feel "stupid" because we don't get straight A's; they make us feel ugly or worthless because we don't have the beautiful faces and looks of the top models and musicians. And then there are the voices of those we opened our hearts to. These voices can be most devastating. They are the ones that tell us they no longer want to be with us. They have met someone else and want to move on.

The evidence of not having self-love is all around us. The evidence is the high rate of teen pregnancy, teen suicide, and drug addiction that has lasted throughout the lifetimes of women and men. I would imagine that not measuring up to the expectations of our parents, peers, significant others, not having a good self-image, and not having self-love are the root cause of these behaviors.

My high school graduation marked a major turning point in my life. When I heard the announcement "The Victor Frankel Scholarship has been awarded to Glenora Yvonne Chandler," I was stunned! I heard my fellow classmates clapping and pushing me to go up to the podium to receive my award. The scholarship was to the Community College of Baltimore. It was an academic scholarship. It meant that my father would not have to worry about paying for my college education for one year. This was one of the greatest accomplishments of my life. I had never done anything that significant in my eighteen years of living. Perhaps I would finally get some recognition, some validation in a family of two brothers and two sisters. Perhaps I would get some validation from my father.

My father was proud that night. However, he still forbade me to hang out with my high school friends after graduation. My staying out late the night before (I had no way of getting home until my friends were ready) was the reason. It seemed to me there was never any understanding or compassion coming from my father. He felt that he had to raise us with an iron fist. I felt he turned a very proud moment into a sad one for me. He never knew how much effort it took for me to even apply and meet with the scholarship committee. I was very shy and introverted throughout most of my life.

So the rebellion started. I got pregnant and left home. I hung out whenever I had the opportunity and when I could find a decent babysitter. I experienced marijuana and other recreational drugs. I struggled for my place in society for a long time. Hurt and resentment can be motivating forces for many of us. The need to prove to others we are more than who they think we are can be very strong. It can drive us to attain and accomplish our personal goals. It can also be the reason that we do harm to ourselves with excessive behaviors such as drinking, using drugs, or being sexually promiscuous. We all need to feel good about ourselves and when we don't we often try to dull our pain.

I never totally understood my mom's over indulgence with alcohol. I used to get so embarrassed when the delivery guy would deliver her the fifth of Madera dark port wine to our home almost every evening. I would cry often when she would fall at home, banging and bruising her body so badly. I remember in my young wisdom cautioning her about the harm she was doing to herself. Still, we would continue to find the glasses of wine hidden in various parts of our home.

But she did stop. I don't know why my mom completely stopped drinking. Perhaps it was the information received after a hospital stay. Perhaps it was the urging of my dad. Perhaps it was her personal embarrassment. I would like to think it was the combination of all three. However, my real belief is that she stopped drinking because of her self-love. I believe the voices that caused her hurt were no longer influencing her. I believed that those voices were replaced by one still, small voice—the voice of God.

I believe that through the voice of God she felt better about her place in society. Because of the strength that she displayed, I found a new sense of strength and self-love. I am over the resentment and hurt of most of my childhood experiences. And I am learning still that when people hurt me in some way, it is really about them, not me. So I forgive them.

I am striving each day to be a better person by refraining from malicious gossiping and taking advantage of people. I learn to put every effort into evaluating my intentions in whatever I do or say each day.

And yes, I still need to be validated to some degree. We all do; it is a human need. However, Quierra, it is the cost of what it takes to have someone love us or accept us. With self-love comes loving the God within you, and his or her still, small voice will speak to you to help you feel good about loving yourself, no matter where you are in life, no matter what you look like, and no matter how smart you are. So love yourself, embrace yourself, and be good to yourself.

Much self-love,
Cookie

CHAPTER IV
Friendship

The reunion of my two very best friends from high school cannot be expressed accurately with words. It was a phone call of a lifetime, a three- way call. When we finally realized that all three of us were conversing at the same time we could not stop laughing and screaming at the top of our lungs. It was hard; however, we all confirmed that we would all be attending the cookout that Juanita was giving a few Saturdays from the date of our initial phone contact.

The time leading up to the cookout had me thinking back to our wonderful and crazy times. Our dreams and goals took us all different directions in life. Our paths rarely crossed in over thirty years. And when our paths would cross, we never seemed to follow through in staying in contact with one another.

Life has a way of making you realize the value of what you hold dear in your heart. I am somewhat saddened to say that it was my sister's illness that prompted me to reconnect with my longtime friend. I knew she was employed at the hospital where my sister was receiving treatment. She received my call with compassion and excitement, and when we added the craziest friend of all to the conversation we realized how much we all still meant to each other.

I am not sure if our spouses really understood our level of excitement prior to our reunion. I think each of us reflected back on the times of yesteryear as often as we were able. Yet the time had finally arrived. And there we were together, once again. It is all so funny to me that my two best friends of high school kept their same boyfriends, now their husbands. I on the other hand, had many. And I had quite a break in between my first marriage, before I married a second time. My two best friends had ten children between the two of them. I had only one child.

Our career paths had similarities in that we all are in a helping profession. The biggest surprise of us all was that our one friend pursued a career in education and is now a principal of a middle school. She was the student who was never sincere about academics. As a matter of fact, my other friend and I were often getting into trouble because of the laughter she often provoked from us when we were in class together. We embraced each other for a long time at the end of the evening and we promised that we would stay in contact with each other more often.

My sister and dad have passed on since our reunion. Both of my very dear friends from high school were also there to console and comfort me through that sad time. However, we have been remiss in staying in contact with one another. I do know that in our hearts and minds we hold much love and mutual respect for each other until the end of time, and we will always be there for each other.

However, my story of friendship does not start and stop with the reunion of my two very dear friends from high school. During those years away from my high school friends, I have worked in corporate America for thirty years. During those thirty years, I have cultivated some true and lasting friendships with at least seven female friends. I smile to myself because it has been miraculous that my friendships with each of these wonderful ladies have become what one of my very best friends, Val, has coined "double-digit friendships." And I cannot leave out my childhood friend, Deborah, who is now a wonderful pastor of a great church. Who would have thought! She has never forgotten my birthday after all of these years and has always been just a phone call away.

Yet each of my wonderful friends have been right there for me in some miraculous way; they have added so much to who I have become today. And though we may not converse each day with each other, we will be right there for each other not only in the sad and troubled times but in the happy and exciting times.

By now you have probably developed relationships with young ladies in your school or neighborhood. You are probably finding that these individuals are fun to be with. You may also find that there are some things that you may tell them that you have absolutely no desire to tell your parents, me, or anyone else.

These things are "secrets" and you have trusted and confided in these friends and have asked them not to tell anyone else what you have told them. But if you learn you have been betrayed and your secret is out, the end result may have been humiliation, embarrassment, and extreme disappointment.

And this, my darling, is one of the first lessons of true friendship. A true friend is someone you can trust with anything you tell him or her. I say "him or her" because you will find that sometime a member of the opposite sex can be equally a good friend. What is important to remember is that friends are people whom you confide in and who confide in you.

As I mentioned earlier, I have many friends and associates. My relationship with each group varies to the extent of what we discuss and share with each other. Within my circle of friends there are two who I know I can share just about anything with. And that does not exclude my two very dear sisters, Gloria and Diane, who also have come to be my dear friends.

What I can say very candidly about friendships is that in order to have good friends you must be a good friend. You must learn to keep the secrets of those who confide in you. That means you keep a secret no matter how juicy or unbelievable it may be. You must be there for them in their time of need too. That means you may have to break a date with your significant other when your friend needs a shoulder to cry on.

As friends we need to look beyond those personality shortcomings; none of us are perfect. True friendship means feeling a sense of accomplishment about the achievements and successes your friends attain in their lives. Envy is natural; however, jealously is very destructive. In the experience of friendship, the green-eyed monster can turn into an ugly and ferocious dragon, looking to destroy and devour you and all that you have worked for.

Here are some of the things your should pay attention to when developing relationships with an individual you think may be a friend: (1) being happy and gloating over the news that your "male friend" is seeing someone else, (2) keeping important information from you that they have knowledge of yet know you are seeking (e.g., job openings, store sales, social events. They want to always have one up on you), (3) seeing them constantly in the faces of members of the opposite sex who have shown an interest in you, not them, yet they are set on discrediting these people just to keep them from being interested in you, (4) spreading malicious gossip about you because of what you look like or what you have, (5) making snide remarks to you about anything you wish to converse about. Pay attention and when you experience some of these issues, reevaluate your relationship with these so-called friends. You may realize that it is time to sever your friendship and move on.

Sometimes we have to move on from the friendships of people we thought would be our friends forever. We may have outgrown them. We may be in a different place in this thing called life. If something has occurred between the two of you and you cannot have a dialogue about the situation, then you are either the guilty party or the one who was the real friend in the relationship, needing that person's validation. Decide what your role is in this relationship and then do what you know in your heart is right. That may mean moving on or ending what you hoped was a true friendship.

I believe that having a friend is a gift from God. Being a friend is a gift to yourself. I have many memories of friendship over the years. One of my dearest ones was when I became pregnant. During this time my friends stayed with me through my nine months of pregnancy and the birth of your father. They supported and encouraged me in many ways. Another wonderful memory is the vote of confidence shared by my friends Pam and Juanita when I was awarded Big Sister of the Year through the Big Brother and Big Sister program. It was no concern of theirs to pay the cost to attend and share in this great award accommodation.

I will never forget the weekend when my very dear friend Shirley flew in from Florida to help me prepare for my wedding. (I don't think I would have walked down the aisle had it not been for her.) During that same time my dear friend Annie gave me a beautiful bridal shower at her home and did all of the preparation.

Obtaining my master's degree was such an accomplishment for me. All of my friends shared this occasion with me in celebration at my son's home. Valerie, Dolores, Annie, Pamela, Sheila (who still calls me her big sis until this day), Juanita, and Wynnie were there. I have to give Dolores her props, because I would involve her in many of my research projects in pursuing this grad degree in gerontology. She was so patient with my interviews.

My friendships have also involved humorous events. Val can confirm that. We have spent many a night on the phone until the wee hours of the morning. Our main topic of interest: "men." For all you men out there, blame Val for why we are no longer together. She got those late night calls, and often when I was sometimes in the most compromising of circumstances!

The saddest times in my life have been the lost of my mother, father, sister, mother-in-law, and father-in-law. But my friends have been right there comforting me, consoling me, and expressing their love for me.

My recent exploits have opened up a new world of people who have been interesting as well as fun. I have formed an alliance with three new friends, one whom I went to school with. (Who would have known?) I am having a great time with these three wonderful ladies: Happy, Darlene, and Tina. Our friendships are evolving each day. And we are learning to trust and share with each other some of our own personal experiences in life.

So remember, Quierra, that when it comes to friendships, you must learn to value the people who are there for you. You must honor them, respect them, and above all, love them unconditionally.

In friendship,
Cookie

CHAPTER V

Health and Hygiene

There are some basic facts that are general knowledge related to good health and hygiene. These are the results of my personal observations and experience. To start, I do believe we are what we eat. In order to be healthy, we need to pay attention to what we consume, how much we consume, and the time we take to consume what we eat.

I am relatively satisfied about my overall body structure and weight. Like any woman, there are some areas that I could improve upon. I would like to eliminate my lower pouch completely! I would also like to have bigger legs and less acne breakouts. But as long as I can continue to turn a few male heads, I feel pretty good!

I would like to say that my overall success for staying healthy is the following:

1. Very little, if any, consumption of red meat.

2. Moderate alcohol consumption. I do drink red wine!

3. Breakfast every morning.

4. Twelve-hour fasts once a week, usually Saturdays.

5. Plenty of exercising. I dance weekly!

6. Meditation—a must! I connect with the God-spirit within and I relieve stress and tension from the day.

7. Good skin care. I am acne-prone due to oily skin.

8. Six to eight glasses of water a day. This helps to regulate my bowels and helps me to decrease any food cravings.

9. Sleep. I strive to sleep seven to eight hours daily.

10. Fruits and vegetables. I try to consume two to three servings of fresh fruit and vegetables five to six times a week.

These are basic for an overall healthy being. However, I want to now focus on health from the female perspective. Even though my mom had breasts and a vagina, she neglected to tell me about some important things in relation to female anatomy and hygiene.

1. As a woman (young woman) you need to pay attention to your breasts. As you get older, you will need to do weekly breast exams to detect any lump or changes in your breasts. These types of exams can be useful in the early stages of breast cancer.

2. Menstruation. This occurs every month until you go through menopause, a time when your period ends. I am there now and I love it!

3. You will probably smell yourself before anyone else. Our bodies do us that favor. Deodorant is an easy fix for underarm odor. However, when it comes to vaginal care, here are some things you need to know:

Douching gives women (young ladies) a sense of cleanliness and freshness. However, as females we tend to "over-douche." Some women feel that douching after menstruation is necessary. Some feel that douching after sexual intercourse is necessary. My personal experience and the experience of my female counterparts is that we tend to over -douche. And as a result, over-douching makes us susceptible to all kinds of vaginitis. Vaginitis is irritation or inflammation of the vagina, the passageway between the uterus and the outside of the body. There are many factors that can cause various kinds of vaginitis:

1. Feminine hygiene spray. It may make us "smell" good; however, it can also lead to burning and irritation of the urethra, the labia minora, and the inner and outer areas of the vagina.

2. Panties that do not have cotton crouches.

3. Jeans that are "too tight," limiting an adequate flow of air.

4. Products such as tampons and soaps.

5. Swimming pools with a high content of chlorine.

6. Ocean water, which has a high content of salt and bacteria.

7. Colored toilet paper, which leads to inflammation of the inner and outer lips.

These are easy fixes. Some of these forms of vaginitis will result in a trip to your GYN physician for a proper medical diagnosis and follow-up treatment. However, there are other types of vaginitis that are actually under the umbrella of STDs (sexually transmitted diseases). I cannot diagnose these, but I do recommend educating yourself about the following STDs and their symptoms:

1. Trichomonas

2. Genital warts, caused by the human papilloma virus

3. Gonorrhea, Syphilis

4. Chlamydia

These are very common and will present symptoms. Please do your own researches, ask questions, and more importantly, pay attention to the following.

1. Do you have a discharge from your vagina that is smelly or causes you to itch?

2. Is the color of your discharge yellow or green? Is it thick and frothy? Is it soaking your panties?

3. Are you experiencing a burning sensation when you urinate? Is there a significant amount of pain in your vagina and pelvic area?

4. Does it hurt when you are having sexual intercourse because of being irritated in the vaginal area?

5. Have you noticed any blisters or a unique growth in or around your genitalia?

Just understand that there are risks associated with sex. One of the greatest risks is having unprotected sex. Knowing some of the risks associated with unprotected sex and being aware of some of the symptoms associated with STDs could be a life-altering experience. The fact is that some STDs can affect your ability to have children. Some STDs even become dormant in you and over time can impact your physical and mental capacity. And over a prolonged period of time, they may even cause your death.

I still cannot get over the lost of my very dear friend. She was a party animal. She would party from dusk to dawn. The news that she had contracted AIDS was earth-shattering to me. I knew about some of her sexual exploits. I still wonder if she contracted the virus from one of them. This was such a delicate matter and one that has remained hush-hush. I learned that the virus was contracted over fourteen years before her death. This left me with a feeling of disbelief. So many people are still having sex on the promise that he or she is "okay." He or she had been tested. However, we still do not ask for concrete evidence. Seeing my friend in her dying days was a wake-up call for me. So many of us still do not realize how devastating and debilitating this illness is.

The fact of the matter is that there are many treatments for many of the STDs. But others you have for the rest of your life. One day a kiss will lead to intimate touching. Intimate touching will lead to oral gratification and actual penetration.

Do not be fooled. Protect yourself, even if he chooses not to protect himself. Wondering and hoping after a night of passion does not overcome the negative consequences. So eat right, exercise, relieve as much stress and tension as possible, and PRACTICE SAFE SEX.

Enjoy life and be safe,
Cookie

Chapter VI
Education

I was so proud to see you reach another major milestone in your life: graduation from middle school. You are on your way. You were very brave during those years, starting a new school and adjusting to a whole new group of students. You did not seem very excited about this new phase of your life. I know that your peers were somewhat intimidating. The environment of middle and high school cannot be imagined. You have to be there, in the middle of it all, to really know how this subculture works. I know. I had a brief year teaching in a middle school. But you made it! And remember, this part of your life is a training ground for your future career endeavors.

A good adage about education that I hold dear to my heart is that education is the key that unlocks all doors. I have seen the impact of how education makes a difference in your career choices. We ask you all the time what you want to be when you grow up. I am sure you are tired of hearing it.

It won't be too far away when you will be relying on your education to get you the job or career of your choice. Don't be fooled into thinking that your education guarantees you a six-figure salary. I'm still waiting! However, your education does guarantee you the kind of job you desire.

It seemed as though I was never going to be in the career of my choice. Being a single mom and getting a job in an industry that guaranteed me a decent salary and good benefits seemed an appropriate alternative. Yet my mind spirit would not let me rest and be contented. Thus, I became a full-time worker during the day and a part-time student in the evening and on the weekends. I needed to keep a roof over my son's and my head. And I wanted to silence the voice in my head. The voice of my father stating I had made a mess out of my life and the odds were totally against me.

Yet I am proud to say that I have earned an AA, BS, and MA, and I have completed an accelerated certification teaching program from a very reputable institution. I am now considering pursuing my PhD.

Through my educational pursuits, I am now an adjunct professor at a university in the city, which I love and enjoy. And I hold a managerial position in a long-term care facility. I spent many nights reading, studying, writing papers, and preparing for exams. Oftentimes, I got in at nights from night school with just a little time left to review and examine my son's - your dad's homework from school. I can remember waking him up and pulling him out of bed to redo homework that was sloppy and incorrect. I even stopped school for a time so that I could effectively get my son through the last three years of high school. However, I did finish my master's program finally in 1991.

What can education do for you? If you really pay attention and stay focused during your English classes, you are guaranteed proficiency in English—speaking and writing. These attributes will benefit you in corporate America to a great extent. The fact of the matter is that being educated offers you the opportunity to having knowledge that can never be taken from you. Please keep in mind that education is not just formal schooling. You can gain a great deal of knowledge by volunteering your services to many organizations that are in need of help. You will gain so much insight into how important it is to give of yourself to make the world a better place.

I will never forget the tug in my heart as a child growing up when I was in the company of an elderly male or female. It seems as though the little old ladies of Westwood Avenue loved having me around. I would always do little errands for them, and I would always be compensated with a few pennies. As I grew older, the desire remained to stay in among the elderly. I did a lot of volunteering in various agencies that dealt with the older population.

My most rewarding experience was with an elderly female of eighty-two years. I served as a friendly visitor to her through the Department of Social Services in Baltimore City. As her companion, I would sit and converse with her about all sorts of things. She was very amusing. I would also accompany her on her doctor appointments, do light shopping for her, and assist her with some aspects of her daily grooming. I can remember being somewhat intimidated by this fair-skinned African American woman with distinct Native American features. She did not show much enthusiasm about me being her companion during our initial introduction. She wondered how I could commit to the two hours every other week. However, as time continued on, my visits to her were met with a great deal of joy and pleasure. We developed a bond of love that lasted until the day she passed away. Today she still lives within me as I continue to contribute to the lives of the elderly.

I implore you to do the same, Quierra. Listen to the urging of your heart. Develop your knowledge and skills through your formal education. However, involve yourself in some type of organization whose goals are to make the world a better place to live in. When you become less selfish and more selfless, you will become a happier, well-rounded, and educated person. Live to give.

Be wise,
Cookie

CHAPTER VII

Love, Sex, and Relationships

It was one of the most romantic times in my life. I will never forget the way he made me feel. He was truly my tall, dark, and handsome man. I allowed him to reach deeply into my heart. Our walks on the beach at nights had been rehearsed so many times in my head with my faceless lover. Now, he was truly here in mind, body, and soul.

I wanted to melt in his arms the first time him and me slow-danced together. There had never been such a feeling of ecstasy. That slow-dance led to many more slow-dances and many more wonderful explosive days and nights that we never wanted to end. We tried to keep the passion going. But our situations and circumstances often led to long breaks in between the times we would finally get together. We had a long-distance love affair. And it would only be a matter of time before our love would be challenged.

I sat in silence for about thirty seconds. He had just explained to me that the female he had just introduced me to upon entering the nightclub was the person he now spent his time with. My first response was that of concern for him. "Are you uncomfortable being here?" There was no reply from him, just a look of stupidity, like the cat who had been caught with the canary in his mouth. Then reality began to set in, with a hint of self-preservation.

So I asked, "Does she know about me?" I began to wonder if I needed to prepare myself for some type of altercation. In other words, I wondered if I would need to get "ghetto fabulous." I wondered whom he would be picking up on the floor—her or me? At that point I demanded to leave; and we did. He must have had his words with her already, because when we left he never said goodbye to her.

The drive to his place was very silent. He finally offered an explanation of who she was and the extent of their involvement. The irony was that he downplayed their relationship. At that point he lost all credibility. What I could not understand was why he had felt the need to lie in the first place. I always encouraged him to be honest about any relationship he would be involved in. Perhaps he felt that his calls for help from time to time would fall on deaf ears if I knew he was in an intimate relationship with another female. You see, he was a struggling single father, and was having some financial and emotional difficulties. I gave him as much as I could emotionally and financially.

When we got back to his place, I drank enough alcohol to knock myself out. I did not want to think or feel anymore. He tried to start the day with some humor about my alcohol consumption the night before. He said I was calling the hogs. I guess I must have snored pretty loudly. However, I was not in a playful mood. I just wanted to get on the train and go back home. You see, I was in a committed relationship at home. I had sought refuge in my lover because I was no longer happy in my relationship. I had hoped that someday he and I would be able to spend the rest of our lives together.

But he lied! My tall, dark, and handsome lover lied. As I took the train ride home the next day, I realized it would be my last time with him. He stayed on the train with me until the whistle sounded. He said, "Cookie, I hope this is not the last time for us. Please forgive me. I am sorry." I embraced him and waved goodbye with tears in my eyes as the train pulled away. I am sure that when he got back to his home he knew the answer. The photograph of him and his son were turned faced down on his bureau. I had left it like that on purpose. I no longer wanted any reminder of him or that night. I never saw him or contacted him after that. I changed all of my phone numbers too. I knew it was time to move on and I did.

And this is a valuable lesson for you about love. KNOW WHEN TO MOVE ON! Don't kid yourself about the basic nature of people. Honesty does count in a relationship. Remember, you will always be able to recover from a broken heart. Just know that at some point in your life, your heart may be broken. But we can survive once we know that it is the experience of being in love that we learn from.

As females we are never without the pressure of when it is appropriate to have sex. This is the year of 2001 and in spite of the many revolutionary changes of society; the burden of when it is appropriate to have sex still falls on women. True, we have evolved sexually as young and older women; we are much more in touch with our sexual beings. I do believe however, that your first sexual encounter will be your decision, not his.

If you do decide to have sex, keep in mind the male and female points of view.

THE MALE POINT OF VIEW

1. He may not ever call you again because this was his only objective for hooking up with you.

2. He may call you on occasion and hope that you will put-out again.

3. He wants you to be committed to him sexually while he still sows his oats.

4. He feels that you have been seeing each other long enough and he should not have to wear a condom anymore.

5. He feels that a blow job should be automatic every time you lie down with him.

6. Love and sex goes together.

7. He believes he owns a part of you now because he has been between your legs.

8. He wants to involve you in one of his sexual fantasies (ménage a trois, bondage, orgies, etc.).

9. He truly loves you and is ready to move forward in the relationship and be sexually exclusive with you.

THE FEMALE POINT OF VIEW

1. You may find that your first sexual experience (sexual intercourse) was nothing like you had expected.

2. You wished you had waited longer for the relationship to develop and now you feel much taken advantage of.

3. He did not use a condom and you spent the next few weeks either worried about being pregnant or having some type of STD.

4. You do not enjoy giving head and wish you had never started this.

5. Size counts.

6. You are insulted. He wants you to fulfill one of his sexual fantasies.

7. You have had the most exhilarating sexual experiences of your life.

8. Love and sex go together.

9. Size does not count.

10. If he asks you to be in an exclusive or committed relationship with him, you will!

Just remember that males and females often come away with two totally different points of view about how and when sex is appropriate. Don't get me wrong, your sexuality is a part of who you are and you should never feel embarrassed by it. You need to discover your body and what makes you feel good. *Self-pleasuring* is not a dirty term.

Just keep in mind that sex does not keep a man in your life. And a blowjob constitutes sex. It is so easy for young and older women to be labeled. I feel that the rules for men and women still apply in the twenty-first century. Men who hop from bed to bed don't seem to mind being labeled as players. Women even in their desire for a variety can be easily considered hoes. Know the rules and accept them. I will not even dismiss the pervasiveness of same-gender relationships. It appears that much of how we view sex and how we express our sexuality is "popular," meaning what everyone else is doing. Don't allow yourself to get caught up in the fads that may haunt you for the rest of your life. And think long and hard about the repercussions.

I have always been a classic romantic. I love the feeling of being in love. I now know that being in love is short-lived. True love comes from accepting each other for who we really are. True love means not judging and expecting others to give to us what it is we cannot give ourselves.

Being in love is different than making a conscious decision to love someone. Fighting the addiction of having passion in my life is an everyday struggle. I have no regrets about my exciting and passionate times with my tall, dark, and handsome man.

Just remember, my darling, that whoever comes into your life should treat you with dignity and respect. You don't need to give him money, buy him gifts, or even do his laundry to keep him in your life. You do not need to clean his house, cook his meals, or satisfy his every sexual desire to keep him in your world.

For me, being a classic romantic has not always been to my detriment. I say that because when the romance dies and true reality sets in, I would come to my senses. By that I mean I did not get overly stupid in my desires to please whoever was in my life. Sure, I did the dinner and movie thing at my expense. I even helped out with some rent and car notes. However, I see so many of my female counterparts totally losing themselves in a man. I have seen them put their careers on hold and have countless children by men who have no thought of taking their hands in marriage. I have even seen them lose all of their material possessions, in addition to having their credit sometimes messed up for a long, long time.

So for love, sex, and relationships, my ending advice is to never totally lose yourself to any one person. Sure, be compassionate, giving, and understanding. But know that you belong to yourself and the universe needs you to do a good thing for it.

Love on,
Cookie

Chapter VIII
Marriage and Family

It is Sunday, September 30, 2001. My mother-in-law is visiting with Craig and me in our beautiful new home in West Virginia. It has been one year since we have been in our new home. We have had both a great and challenging year. You see, my mother-in-law is terminally ill. She is dying. My dad, as you know, passed away in March of this year. My sister Doris is still recovering from a stroke.

I have never realized how important family is until I have grown older. When we are young, we tend to take the people who are always around for granted. The day my dad passed away was so symbolic of how I had evolved in my relationship with him. I smile about how brash and honest he was, very often offending those in his line of fire. I am similar to him to a degree now, in my honesty and candidness about issues.

I hated his strict ways when growing up. All of my sisters and brothers were fearful of him. My mom's threat of "I am going to tell your father on you when he gets home" was an effective measure of keeping us in line. And yet I was there for him in his final days. I took him to his doctor's visits. My sister Sissy and I would pick Daddy up and take him to various family events. Craig and I looked forward to inviting him to our annual Father's Day cookouts each year. Our roles were changing as he got older and we got older. Thankfully Daddy did not have an illness that caused long suffering and required a lot of time and planning on the family's behalf. Mommy, on the other hand, did.

Mommy's diagnosis of Alzheimer's dementia was very challenging and stressful on the family. The responsibilities of helping to keep her from being in a nursing home in her last dying days were not equally shared by my siblings. I resented the lack of their involvement. I did all I could. When we finally had a plan in place to bring her home, she passed away. Perhaps in her own spirit, she did not want to be a burden.

So here I am, faced again with another family member's illness—my mother-in-law's. Craig and his brother have been very, very caring. However, I bear a great brunt of his hurts. Men are not taught to share their feelings. So when he comes home tired from caring for his mom hands-on, it does not take much to set him off.

When we marry the man or woman of our dreams, we also marry their families and all of the trying and challenging situations that come with that family. That means we marry the busy-body, meddling mother-in-law, the nosy aunt or uncle, the drug-addicted cousin, the alcoholic niece or nephew, and the snooty sister-in-law. We have to respect each of these family members' own rights, and often we are not able to. As a result, we have a great deal of conflict over other people we had not considered when we made the decision to marry someone.

Recent statistics indicate that 50 percent of marriages now end in divorce. In the 50 percent of marriages that end in divorce, children are involved. With children come nasty custody hearings, alimony, and child support. Too often women are using their children as pawns between them and their spouses.

Men are not standing up for the rights to see their children and so they disappear off of the scene forever. They feel that the courts are not on their side. Do they not realize the impact of their desertion on young boys and girls around the world?

My first marriage was in a courthouse. I was seven months pregnant. My dad did not want me to bring shame to the family, so I married your dad's father. We had an amicable marriage in the very beginning. We were introduced to each other by mutual friends. He appeared to be one of the better guys in the neighborhood. I felt so sorry for him at first. He lived in a foster home all of his younger life. When I met him, he was still in a foster home. His mother was an alcoholic. During the time she became involved in our lives she had recovered and no longer drank.

I stayed in this marriage for about one year. I knew it was time to go when I defended myself with the sparerib I was thawing out for dinner. I ran him around the house with it. He had become abusive. It only takes one hit to know that another one is coming. With pent-up anger and frustrations, someone will ultimately be hurt. We were both suffering from the hurts of our childhood. I knew it was time to go.

Through the years I have learned that so many of us bring a lot of unrequited hurts in our marriages. We expect the people we marry to make us feel better about ourselves. That is our challenge, not theirs. I often hear the term *dysfunctional family* used to describe the many types of families in existence today. *Dysfunctional* means that if there is not a father or mother in the home with the 2.5 children, your family structure is not normal. What I now know to be true is that not everything that looks good on the outside is working well on the inside. Being raised by a single mother or father does not negate your chances into making something great of your life. True, you may not reap all of the benefits that one would hope come from having two parents at home, but you learn to make the best of your situation. I know several two-parent homes where love and mutual respect are absent. So if you have one parent who is doing everything he or she can, appreciate him or her.

I also know that family is not only two people who are connected through blood or bloodlines. Family members are the wonderful people who have fulfilled the roles of mother, father, sister, brother, and cousin in our lives. They are known as our "fictive kin." They are the ones who show up at our times of need. They are the ones who have the opened ears and hearts. Value the family that you have. Take some time out to call them and let them know you love and appreciate what they do for you.

Sissy and I have invested a lot of time, money, and effort in the lives of you, Devin, and Chris. We have taken you on great vacations every year. What do we hope to gain from our investments? We would hope that our time, kindness, and effort are reciprocated when you become productive members of society. We want to be rewarded through your completion of high school, college, and your great careers. When you marry and have your own families, we want invitations to your Thanksgiving dinners, Christmas/ Kwanza, and New Year's celebrations, but we mainly want you all to take us on the vacation of our lives!

I am now in my second marriage, and I have married a great guy. We have had our ups and downs; however, we have endured. If I am asked at the end of the day what it is that a woman wants in a relationship, particularly in a marriage, I would have to say a woman wants security. That is not to say that she does not want to have love and respect, but at the end of the day she wants the feeling that you, as her man, can come through for her. And this is why I am still married fifteen years into this marriage. We have knock-down arguments (no physical blows), we have our doors slamming, and we may even sleep in separate rooms at times. But I know that Craig has and will come through for me and I have always and will come through for him. Do I get attracted to other men? No doubt! Does he get attracted to other women? No doubt! However, I do not spend sleepless nights worrying about that. As long as I feel secure in this marriage, he will have me for the rest of his life. Why not? I am the best thing that ever happened to him!

So Quierra, whenever you do decide to get married and have a family, know that you are marrying not just your man but his family. There are many reasons people get married today. Not all of them are good reasons. There are many reasons marriages end today. Infidelity, finances, and abuse are the main three reasons. So get some counseling before you marry. Take the time to know and understand the person you will be sleeping with each night. Get to know his family. And never rush into such a life-altering decision.

In hope,
Cookie

CHAPTER IX

Money / Money Management

As I sit on the balcony of our beautiful timeshare property in Freeport, Bahamas, I've come to realize five very important things about money. They are: (1) without money, your opportunities in life can be limited, (2) good credit is the key to buying those big-ticket items: home, car, financing your education, (3) a good number of us in American society are just one paycheck away from being homeless, (4) a good number of us in American society are overwhelmed with debt and are having a hard time trying to get from under it, and (5) there is a spiritual component to money, which entails giving to receive. I will explain each.

I grew up without a lot of extravagances. My mother worked as a domestic worker and she cooked and cleaned in the homes of others. My dad was a cook by profession. Thus, our opportunities were limited in what my parents could afford for us. Most of our wonderful outings (e.g., amusement parks, beaches, picnics, etc.) were through our church. As we grew older, my dad felt that my mom should stay at home to watch our going and coming. We sat in the dark many a night until my dad could afford to have the gas and electricity turned on. As children we thought this to be a fun event because we were guaranteed steak subs brought home at nights by my dad for dinner. Eating carry-out food was a luxury item for us (imagine). It was not until my long walk home with my mom in one hundred-degree weather that the realization of having little money hit me.

I saw my mom turn her pocket book upside down to pay the last six cents for the gas and electric bill. She spent our carfare, and we had to walk all of the way home from downtown Baltimore. We lived on the west side of town. Our trip was stopped every few blocks to sit on someone's steps so that I could regain my momentum for more miles ahead. During our walk home, we spotted an ice-cream truck. My mom seemed elated when she dug into her pocket and found five cents to buy a Popsicle for me. It was an orange one, my favorite. I was so delighted to have that refreshment. When we finally made it home, I went straight to bed. It was about two in the afternoon.

As a single mom, I vowed that my son would never have that type of experience. I worked full- and part-time to keep a roof over our heads. In addition, I had the help of my two sisters when it was time for school shopping and my son's other needs. I involved your dad in all of the activities I could. He took piano lessons. He was sent to camp each summer, he participated in programs at the YMCA, and he even took karate lessons. I wanted him to have all of the opportunities that I missed out on. And I wanted to make him as well rounded as possible.

As my wants for him increased, my wants for myself did. I wanted the best clothes with the designer names, nice cars to drive, vacations to go on, etc. As you see, even though I had a good job, my wants exceed my needs. And often, when our wants exceed our needs, we paid dearly for them. Because then we start acquiring everything through credit. As I stated, good credit is essential for some of the big-ticket items that we have; however, one day we wake up and we realize we don't even know what we have bought when the big credit cards and other bills come in. Many of us file for bankruptcy because of our enormous debts.

I have come a long way since the time of my ducking phone calls and ignoring threatening letters. I began to read and pay attention to information about getting out from under my debts. So many of us end up in these dire situations as a result of losing our jobs, ending our marriages, or having some catastrophic illness concerning either ourselves, or our children or other loved ones. So my advice to you now is to begin to save a little of what you have each time you get paid. Once you become established in a career, contribute to your company's savings plan (401K). Educate yourself about the differences between mutual funds, the stock market, annuities, and interest rates.

I thought I was set for life when I left my former place of employment. I chose to take my pension in a lump sum and live off of the interest generated each month from the principal amount. The principal amount was to generate enough interest that I could still live comfortably each month. The country was experiencing a good time economically. We were what were called by the experts in a "bull" market. I was never so ill advised. Two major events occurred that shook the foundation of many of us who had investments we thought were relatively safe. They were the attacks of 911 and the Enron scandal. I saw my financial portfolio take a nosedive I never imagined. It was time to seek another advisor to keep what I had left, and I did.

I am now working full-time again. I have always had my education to fall back on. It was easy for me to get a job in my profession. I managed to keep my credit well established. Fortunately for me, I had a husband who was in a good profession. However, there is still one more component that I believe has helped me maintain financial stability. And it is a very controversial issue. You see, I tithe.

I believe there is a spiritual component to everything we do in life. If I were asked if I am a religious person, I would say I am to some degree. As you have likely noted, I have not dwelled on the topic of religion. How you choose to worship is your personal choice. In the first chapter I discussed the source within because I believe we are all spiritual beings and who and how we worship is very cultural. But I also believe that there is a spiritual principle in giving and it does not matter what your religion is.

I read and researched religions all over the world. And I found the same underlying message about what you do and how you give in life. In other words, we reap what we sow. Therefore, if you are giving little in life (and giving encompasses many things), you are going to receive little back. I believe this applies to money as well. I tithe financially because I believe it is necessary for kingdom building. Kingdom building is helping my church in obtaining its goals for community and outreach programs and compensating the pastor's efforts to help the parishioners; and I tithe for the maintenance and improvement of the structural conditions of the church. I can truly say my financial picture has improved since I began to tithe. True, I still have outstanding debts, but I am slowly eliminating them and my goal is to be debt-free in three years. I have even acquired another home since I first began to write this book.

Don't let anyone tell you that money is the root of all evil. It is the love of money that causes all of the evil, underhanded, and diabolical occurrences in the world. It is the greed that has made so many people in power make six- and seven-figure salaries while the masses struggle to keep the basics going. Our reference points are those we see in the sports world, in Hollywood, and in the music industry. We want to have what they have, hoping that we will be happy for the rest of our lives. And this is my final point regarding money: MONEY WILL NOT BUY YOU HAPPINESS AND MONEY WILL NOT BUY YOU LOVE.

I will not deny that I feel so much better about life when my bills are paid on time, when I can take a vacation that I will not have to charge with a credit card, and when I take you guys to West Virginia and pay cash for all of your wants and needs. However, I know that it is not the acquisition of things that brings true happiness, for the more we have, the more we want. I had hoped that before you graduated from high school I would have enough money saved to pay for a large portion of your education as well as have a new car waiting for you when you left the graduation ceremony. I have kept the promise of taking you on an exotic vacation. One of the purposes of this book is to help pay for your college education. Who knows? Maybe I can make good on the other two goals.

In closing, I just want to say be wise with the money you have and the money you will make. Educate yourself more each day about how to make and manage your money. Understand that things only bring temporary fulfillment. They are not what we really need in life. And finally, understand that we are all spiritual beings. What we get in life is often what we give.

Spend wisely,
Cookie

CHAPTER X
Death

The death of Melvin was my first earth-shattering experience of losing a loved one. The news that he had been shot was shocking. I had just left my ex-mother-in-law's home. She agreed to watching Tony (your dad) so I could attend Morgan State home-coming dance. My mother-in-law appeared shocked as she ran down the street to give me the news. I will never forget her words. She said: "Cookie, your mother is on the phone. It's about Melvin. Melvin's been shot."

Melvin and I lived together for a few years. He was a wonderful father to Tony-your dad. He had no children of his own. He became abusive after awhile in our relationship; because of that I moved out on my own. He appeared to be getting himself together. Before my trip to my ex-mother-in-law's home I had a conversation with Melvin. Our conversation was about Tony. He said he missed him and he asked me if I would agree to allow Tony to spend next weekend with him. I agreed. Melvin was shot the very same weekend.

Since the time of my first chapter to now, several close family members have passed on. Some of these people were my mother, your grandmother, my dad (grandpa), my sister, your father's dad, and Craig's mom and dad. It seemed as though I was never going to stop going to funerals. I am sure you felt that way too. I saw some of the hurt and sadness in your eyes.

I had somewhat of a difficult time with mommy's passing. I would visit her graveside often, or ride through the cemetery just to feel her presence. On one particular afternoon I felt an urging to visit daddy. I wanted to see how he was coming along after mommy's passing. He was sitting in his usual chair by the window. I noticed he had been crying. Daddy always had a strong demeanor; we rarely saw his soft side. On that particular day however, he did not seem to mind showing that side. We talked for awhile about mommy. I left about two hours later. It seemed as though my visit was divinely timed.

That night I remembered awakening from my own cries of missing mommy. I then felt the side of my bed go down as if someone were sitting on it. I realized that it was mommy sitting on the side of my bed. I began to cry harder. I told her that I loved and missed her. I said my life would never be the same with her gone. In the midst of my tears, I noticed mommy had a beautiful presence. Her body was no longer contorted and twisted. Her silver hair had been bright and shiny. Mommy always had a way of talking in amusing terms and this night was no exception. She told me she was fine and she asked me to stay strong. She also asked me to continue to look out for daddy. I continued to cry after she left only to be shaken by Craig. He asked me if I were "alright." He said, "I think you are having a bad dream." I told him I had just had a visit from mommy. Was it a dream? Perhaps it was. I do know that after that experience I did not have the feeling of despair from mommy's passing as before. I felt a sense of peace that is difficult to explain. I no longer felt lost and abandoned.

Death is no surprise to us on this planet. We all know that we all have to leave our present existence someday. It is just the timing of certain deaths that catch us with such grief. Various cultures have different views about what happens to us when we are no longer in the present. It is these religious beliefs and philosophies that greatly influence our preparation for what happens to us when we die.

Some cultures and belief systems feel that we come back in our next life to atone for all of the wrong we have done in the previous life. Other belief systems argue that we come back many times until we reach a level of perfection and never have to come back again. Other belief systems argue that we have to live a life so that we can be judged accordingly. And if our works done on this earth are approved by our Supreme Being, we are allowed to live in heaven and see and greet those who have gone on before us. If we don't strive to live a good life and if we don't be kind and understanding to mankind, we will be judged by our actions, which may ultimately mean we are dammed throughout eternity and will burn in hell forever.

Your philosophy about life and death and what will happen to you is something that will come as a result of your education, your life experiences, and what you have been taught. And it could be a combination of all three. I believe we create our own heaven on this earth and we create our own hell. The most important thing I think to keep in mind about death is your life preceding it. By this I mean live for today as if you don't have tomorrow. I don't mean squander everything you have, throw caution to the wind, and be stupid about your actions. If you do that you will have to suffer the consequences. What I mean is stretch your imagination and follow your dreams. Say goodbye to any behaviors that impinge your growth. Look your fears in the eyes and tell them "Hasta la vista, baby."

I am having the time of my life now. I am teaching, traveling, dancing, and meeting new people every day. Each day I go into my workplace, I am making a difference, either through a smile, a touch, or a conversation. But more importantly, I am writing this book as a dedication to you.

Whatever happens to us after we pass on is not totally certain to anybody. Is there a guardian angel walking with us each day, protecting us, guiding us, intervening on our behalf until our number is up? If there is, I know mine is working overtime. I am convinced that I am loved by the universe, and in whatever way I choose to live my life, (and I do strive to do the best, but I am a free spirit and sometimes live by my own rules) I will have few, if any, regrets when my time on this planet has run its course. When you have come close to death, as I have, you learn to appreciate life much more. You learn to face whatever obstacles come your way. And you learn to appreciate and respect all who have come into your life. So my darling, live your life and love all that it has to offer you.

Live on!
Cookie

Closing and Acknowledgments

It is such a rewarding experience to know that I have finally ended this project. It has been nine years in the making. I have covered what I think are some valuable truths and perspectives on what life is about and how these truths may help you in this journey. True, life is not easy. I, along with others, have often asked our God, Why did you make it so rough? But we know that a lot of what we go through and will go through is the result of our own thoughts and actions. We also know that we have to accept and deal with whatever comes our way, even if we have had no direct influence.

I hope I have given a voice to the grandmothers who through their tireless efforts can affirm and relate to some of my views and perspectives on this journey called life. I hope that grandfathers will also embrace my perspectives and views. And for mothers and fathers, aunts and uncles, I hope you too will find some value in this written work. Know that I am no person of great significance. This is not a book people of great minds may even be interested in. I am not a Hollywood starlet or a musician, and I don't have masses of people who run behind me just to have me touch them or acknowledge them in some way. This is also not a book about true confessions. Yes, I have many secrets that I will take to the grave.

But I am a grandmother. And I believe I am and will continue to be a good one. And I have lived a life and have had experiences that may help my granddaughter to become and achieve anything she wants to achieve in life. This is not reflection on any of the wonderful people in her life now: her parents, aunts, uncles, friends, etc. This is my life and my perspectives.

My role as a grandmother is continuing to evolve since the inception of this project. I have been blessed by the birth of a grandson, who is now three; and have learned a new grandchild is on the way. And you have finished high school, Quierra. You are now starting college.

So many people have inspired me along my life's journey. For in this journey, we need to know and understand how others have fulfilled their dreams and goals, faced their obstacles, and gotten rid of their fears. They have helped me get where I am today. They are Marilyn McCoo, Oprah Winfrey, Maya Angelou, Dr. Johnnetta Cole, Sanaya Roman, Iyanla Vanzant, Catherine Ponder, Dr. Wayne Dyer, Neale Donald Walsch, Norman Vincent Peale, Dr. M. Scott Peck, Rev. Jim Holley, Rev. Joel Olsteen, and my pastor, Rev. Dr. Charles Coger. There are so many more; however, these are just a few of the people who through some venue have been so inspirational in my life and have helped me stay on course.

I will also like to thank my husband Craig, who left me alone to write and type this book, sometimes until the wee hours of the morning. I want to thank all of my friends, male and female, whom I have learned so much from. You have graced my life when I needed you in very important ways. I especially thank D.J. Slice (Craig Cole), who has been playing my music for years. There are not enough words to thank my sister Dee Dee, who took on the task of typing most of the manuscript of this book. She had the difficult task of deciphering my handwriting. She has a book on its way too (she just doesn't know it yet). I want to also thank my brother-in-law Drake for the cover photographs.

And last but not least, I want to thank my dear Quierra. You are the inspiration for this book. I have watched how you have found a place within yourself to be safe. In spite of your shyness you have faced some of your obstacles very bravely. You have endured family crises in a way that us grown folk could never have done. You have a beautiful inner spirit that will take you to heights you have never dreamed of. I am sure you have a guardian angel walking near you and protecting you each day. But trust that when my present time ends and I transcend to my next life, I will also be there watching over you and looking out for you for the rest of your life. Thank you for being who you are in my life.

The End

www.ingramcontent.com/pod-product-compliance
Lightning Source LLC
Chambersburg PA
CBHW031250280526
45784CB00004B/1791